THE APOSTLES' CREED

THE

APOSTLES' CREED

BY

ADOLF HARNACK

A TRANSLATION FROM AN ARTICLE IN THE
THIRD EDITION OF HERZOG'S REALENCYCLOPÄDIE

BY THE

REV. STEWART MEANS

REVISED AND EDITED BY

THOMAS BAILEY SAUNDERS

Wipf and Stock Publishers
150 West Broadway • Eugene OR 97401
2001

The Apostles' Creed

By Harnack, Adolf

ISBN: 1-57910-663-3

Reprinted by *Wipf and Stock Publishers*
150 West Broadway • Eugene OR 97401

Previously published by Adam and Charles Black, 1901.

THE APOSTLES' CREED [1]

THE first to place the three creeds, the
Apostolic, the Nicene-Constantinopolitan,
and the Athanasian, side by side, as a full

[1] Notwithstanding the earlier labours of Laurentius
Valla and Erasmus, the writer who may be described as
the pioneer in the branch of investigation which deals
with the origin of the creeds in the ancient Church is
Usher, *De Romanae ecclesiae symbolo apostolico vetere
aliisque fidei formulis tum ab occidentalibus tum ab
orientalibus in prima catechesei et baptismo proponi
solitis Diatriba*, 1647. Next come. the names of
Vossius, Pearson, Witsius, King, and Bingham. Walch
collected the "Rules of Faith and the Symbols" in his
Biblioth. Symbol. vetus, in 1770. His work was superseded in 1842 by Hahn's *Bibliothek*. During the last
forty-three years a fresh interest has been given to this
field of labour by Heurtley's *Harmonia Symbolica*

expression of the ecumenical confessions
in the Church (with the addition of the
Te Deum Laudamus) was probably Luther.
Certain it is that it was only after his time,

(1858).   More particularly since the year 1866, Caspari,
a second Usher, has, by his various works, enormously
increased the material for a study of this subject, and he
has also sifted the material with the most critical care,
*Ungedruckte, unbeachtete und wenig beachtete Quellen
zur Geschichte des Taufsymbols und der Glaubensregeln,*
3 Bde., 1866-69-75 ; *Alte und neue Quellen zur Geschichte
des Taufsymbols und der Glaubensregeln*, 1879.   His
labours enabled Hahn's son to make a new work of his
father's *Bibliothek* in 1877.   Among German scholars,
von Zezschwitz, *System der Katechetik*, 2 Bde., 2te Auf.
1872, the present writer in the second edition of the
Realencyclopädie and in the first volume of his *Dog-
mengeschichte*, Zahn, *Das apostolische Symbolum*, and
above all, Kattenbusch, have taken a share in these investigations.   In 1894 the last-named writer issued the
first volume of a great monograph upon the Creed, which
justifies the eagerness with which its continuation is
awaited.   Among English scholars may be mentioned
Harvey, *The History and Theology of the Three Creeds*,
1854 ; Foulke, *The Athanasian Creed . . . with other
Inquiries on Creeds in General*, 1872 ; Lumby, *The*

that is, after the second half of the sixteenth century, that Protestants first spoke definitely of the three ancient symbols. Yet it is also certain on the other hand that in the West these very three symbols had been in use in the churches, and had enjoyed great consideration, at least as much as five centuries earlier.[1] In the strict sense of the word, however, the predicate " ecumenical " applies only to the

History of the Creed, 1873 ; Hort, *Two Dissertations*, 1876 ; and, above all, Swainson, *The Nicene and Apostles' Creed*, London, 1875. The relation of the old Roman symbol to the Formulas of Faith in the pre-Catholic period has been treated by the present writer in his *Patr. App. Opp.* ii. edit. 1, 2, 1878 (cf. A. Harnack, *Das apostol. Glaubensbekenntniss*, 26ᵗᵉ Auf. 1893). Reference should also be made to the text-books on the History of Dogma. In the controversies periodically occurring over the Apostles' Creed a great number of brochures regularly appear which need not be enumerated here.

[1] Köllner, *Symbolik*, i. ed. 1837, p. 5.

Nicene-Constantinopolitan Creed, for in
the Eastern Church neither the Apostolic
nor the Athanasian confession of faith
has at any time received official recogni-
tion.[1]   Indeed, the Eastern Church has at
no time traced any creed to an Apostolic
origin, or designated any as Apostolic in
the strict sense of the word.[2]   In the West,
on the other hand, the three symbols form
part of the confessional writings of the
main Church, and the shortest of them
(*Symbolum minus*) bears the very name
"Apostolicum."   But we also find the

[1] Gass, *Symbolik d. griech. Kirche*, 1872, pp. 116 ff.;
Kattenbusch, *Das apost. Symbol.* Bd. i. S. 1, 1894.

[2] Cf. the testimony of Archbishop Marcus Eugenicus
at the Council of Florence, in 1438, as given by Sylvester
Sguropolis, *Hist. Concil. Florent.* sect. vi. c. 6, p. 150,
edit. Rob. Creyghton, 1660: ἡμεῖς οὔτε ἔχομεν, οὔτε
οἴδαμεν σύμβολον τῶν ἀποστόλων.   *Vide* Caspari, *Ungedruckte . . . Quellen z. Gesch. des Taufsymbols*, ii.
1869, S. 106 ff.

name "Apostolic" here and there established and in use in the West as a designation of the Nicene-Constantinopolitan Creed;[1] nor is this only among Greeks who had become latinised. The three chief churches of the West possess the Symbolum Apostolicum in a form which agrees in all essential points ("Textus Receptus"). We shall therefore have to begin by treating of the origin of the creed in this form.

I

THE "Textus Receptus" can, with a satisfactory degree of certainty, be traced back, except in certain minute details, to the beginning of the sixth, or to the end of the fifth century. But there is a strong

[1] Caspari, *ibid.* i. 1866, S. 242, n. 45; ii. 1869, S. 115, n. 88; iii. 1875, S. 12, n. 22.

probability that this form of the symbol was not previously in official use in any church, whether as a part of the *Interrogationes de fide* or the *Traditio* and *Redditio Symboli;* nay, there is no discoverable sign of the existence of this particular form before the middle of the fifth century.[1] As it did not, at all events, come to the West from the Eastern Church, and symbols can be shown to have been in use in various provincial churches in the West during the fourth and fifth centuries which materially differ from the " textus receptus " of the Apostolicum, we may infer that it scarcely existed in its received form earlier than the middle of the fifth century, and probably did not assume its present shape,

[1] Kattenbusch, *ibid.* S. 189 ff., who curiously disputes this view, has hitherto only partly stated his reasons for dissenting from it.

complete in every detail, before about the year 500. In that shape it appears for the first time in a sermon of Caesarius of Arles.[1] The immediate predecessor of Caesarius' symbol, or, as the case may be, of the Apostolicum as we have it, is very probably that of Faustus of Rietz, about 460, but it does not admit of being satisfactorily reconstructed.[2] On the other hand the stage succeeding that of the old Roman symbol in the direction of our Apostles' Creed is represented by the highly interesting symbol discovered by Bratke in the Berne Codex,[3] which I regard with him as a Gallican, or, as the

---

[1] Pseudo-Augustin. n. 244, *vide* Kattenbusch, *ibid.* S. 164 ff., cf. also *Sermo* 240 and 241 ; the texts are in Hahn's *Bibliothek der Symbole*, 2te Auf. 47-49, and the symbol is in the *Missale Gallicanum vetus* (Hahn, § 36).

[2] Hahn, 38 ; Kattenbusch, S. 158 ff.

[3] N. 645, saec. vii. (*StK.* 1895, S. 153).

case may be, a Gallico-British symbol, and
assign to the fourth century. It differs
from the old Roman symbol only by the
additions of "passus," "descendit ad
inferos," "catholicam," and "vitam aeternam." These four additions all lie in
the direction of our Apostles' Creed and
at the same time prove that they are
the four oldest additions, whilst "conceptus, etc." and "communionem sanctorum" are later.   "Creatorem coeli et
terrae" and "mortuus" are also earlier.[1]

Against the Roman origin of the
Apostles' Creed, called by modern writers
the later and longer Roman symbol, inas-
much as it was undoubtedly through the
influence of Rome that it in later times

[1] That the Greek texts of the Gallicanum-textus
receptus are translations, no one disputes (Hahn, §§ 47β,
49).   As to these texts, cf. Caspari, *Quellen z. Geschichte
des Taufsymbols*, Bd. iii.

attained universal authority in the West, we may oppose the fact (1) that it was not found in Rome until the Middle Ages, that is to say, many centuries after its existence had been attested by Caesarius of Arles, and (2) that from the end of the fifth, or the beginning of the sixth century, until the tenth, the Nicene-Constantinopolitan Creed in Greek, and the Apostles' Creed, were used in Rome in the *traditio symboli*,[1] and that, so far as the use of a shorter symbol side by side with the Constantinopolitan was known in Rome during the Byzantine period (the sixth to the eighth century), it was not identical with the Apostles' Creed. Our Apostles' Creed points very plainly to Southern Gaul, and to a period about the year 500. But the spread of the "textus receptus"

[1] Caspari, iii. S. 201 f., 226, ii. S. 114 f. n. 88.

of the Symbolum Apostolicum throughout
Western Europe in the sixth century was
soon accompanied by the legend of its
wonderful origin.[1]   That a symbol of
such recent origin should from the beginning bear the name "Apostolic" sug-
gests the conjecture that it has a history
earlier than the fifth century, and that
another form must have preceded the
"textus receptus," the attributes of which
were then transferred to the new text
supplanting it.   The contention that this
later creed or symbol traced its origin to a
συμβολή or "collatio" involves a confusion
between συμβολή, which also bears the
meaning of "summa" or "brevis com-
plexio," and σύμβολον, that is, "signum,"
"indicium," in the sense not only of a
distinction between Christians and non-

[1] Hahn, § 46 β.

Christians, or between Christians and heretics, but also in the sense of "tessera militum," a token or deed of agreement.[1] The name "Symbolum" is first found in the West in Cyprian;[2] in the East, not until after the beginning of the sixth century.[3] The legend[4] that each of the twelve Apostles, in a general session before their separation, contributed a phrase to the creed, was exploded even as early as Laurentius Valla and Erasmus,[5] but seems

---

[1] Caspari, ii. S. 88.

[2] *Ep.* 69 *ad Magnum*, c. 7.

[3] Caspari, i. S. 24 f. n. 28.   As to the various designations of the creed, cf. Caspari, i. S. 21 f. n. 26, iii. S. 30 ; Nitzsch, *ZThK.* Bd. iii. S. 332 ff.; Kattenbusch, S. 1 ff., S. 37 ff.; *Lehrbuch der vergleichenden Konfessionskunde*, Bd. i. S. 5 ff.

[4] Hahn, § 47 f.; Köllner, *ibid.* S. 7 f.; Caspari, ii. S. 93 f.

[5] Monrad, *Die erste Kontroverse über d. Ursprung des apost. Glaubensbekenntnisses* ; Kattenbusch, *Apost. Symb.* S. 1 ff.   The Roman Catechism has nevertheless retained it.

to point to a confirmation of the conjecture above hazarded as to the earlier form. This conjecture, which is also suggested by a glance at the very simple contents of the creed and its clear and compact form, is strikingly confirmed by history.

II

THE fact that the Roman Church in the period between 250 and 460 A.D., and partly also later,[1] used a symbol in its religious services which was held in very great honour and to which no additions were permitted, has been well known ever since Usher's investigations,[2] but was more particularly proved by Caspari's researches. At Rome this symbol was believed to have been obtained from the Apostles in the form in which it was used, and this led to the supposition that Peter brought it to Rome. The idea of its Apostolic origin

[1] *Vide* Gregory the Great.   [2] Usher, *op. cit.*

did not arise later than the fourth century. We find this symbol, the older, shorter Roman creed, existing complete in a number of texts,[1] quite independently of the sources from which it could be at least partially reconstructed.

[1] A few of the more important of these texts may be here named : a Greek text in the Epistle of Marcellus of Ancyra to the Roman bishop, Julius, about the year 337 or 338 A.D. (*Epiphan. Panar. haer.* 52 (72), *Opp.* T. i. p. 836, ed. Petav.; Hahn, *ibid.* § 15 ; Caspari, *op. cit.* iii. S. 4 f., S. 28-161), and also in a MS. of the Biblioth. Cottoniana, the so-called *Psalterium Aethelstani*, saec. ix. (Hahn, § 16 ; Caspari, iii. S. 5 f., S. 161-203). The Latin text is in the Codex Laudianus 35, in the Bodleian Library, belonging to the sixth or seventh century (Caspari, iii. S. 162 f.; Hahn, § 17); also in a MS. in the British Museum, 2 A, xx., of about the eighth century (Swainson, *The Nicene and Apostles' Creeds*, 1875, p. 161 f.); in the *Explanatio Symboli ad initiandos*, attributed to Ambrose or, as the case may be, to Maximus of Turin (A. Mai, *Script. Vet. Nova Coll.* T. vii. p. 156 f. 1883), B. Brunus, Maximi Tur. *Opp.* p. 30 f., 1784 ; Hahn, § 20 ; Caspari, ii. S. 48 ff., who makes it probable that the treatise came from Ambrose.

The Greek text must be regarded as the original, for at Rome the symbol was for a long time used only in Greek.[1] It was not until long after the Greek text was in use that the Latin text was adopted as a parallel form. What happened here, then, is just the opposite of what happened in the case of the longer symbol.[2] The

Against this view Kattenbusch urges some weighty considerations, which, however, do not seem to me conclusive ; cf. also in Rufin. *Expos. in Symb. Apost.* in *Opp. Cypr.* Append. ed. Fell, p. 17 f. 1682 ; see Hahn, 14 ; and also the so-called Florentine Symbol ; Caspari, iv. S. 290 ff.; and some statements in the 24th epist. of Leo the Great (Hahn, § 18).

[1] See the reconstruction of the text in my treatise upon the old Roman Symbol (*Patr. Apost. Opp.* 2 edit. I, 2, 1878), and more especially in Kattenbusch's programme, *Beitr. z. Gesch. des altkirchl. Taufsymbols*, Giessen, 1892 ; also his *Apost. Symbol.* S. 59 ff., where a recension of the Latin text is also given. The best authorities are the *Psalterium Aethelstani* on the one side, and the Codex Laudianus on the other.

[2] On the use of Greek in the Roman Church, cf. Caspari, iii. S. 267-466 ; upon the liturgical use of the

following is the text of the shorter or Greek form : Πιστεύω εἰς θεὸν πατέρα παν-τοκράτορα καὶ εἰς Χριστὸν Ἰησοῦν (τὸν) υἱὸν αὐτοῦ τὸν μονογενῆ, τὸν κύριον ἡμῶν, τὸν γεν-νηθέντα ἐκ πνεύματος ἁγίου καὶ Μαρίας τῆς παρθένου, τὸν ἐπὶ Ποντίου Πιλάτου σταυρωθέντα καὶ ταφέντα, τῇ τρίτῃ ἡμέρᾳ· ἀναστάντα ἐκ (τῶν) νεκρῶν, ἀναβάντα εἰς τοὺς οὐρανούς, καθήμενον ἐν δεξιᾷ τοῦ πατρὸς ὅθεν ἔρχεται κρῖναι ζῶντας καὶ νεκρούς, καὶ εἰς πνεῦμα ἅγιον, ἁγίαν ἐκκλη-σίαν, ἄφεσιν ἁμαρτιῶν, σαρκὸς ἀνάστασιν.

The legend of the symbol having been composed by the Apostles appears as early as the above-mentioned *Explanatio Symboli* of Ambrose.   The fact that the writer was aware of its being divided into twelve articles perhaps indicates that the legend of each Apostle having contributed one of

Greek text in the West during the early Middle Ages, cf. *ibid. passim*, and iii. 466-510.

them was already known. The twelve
articles were arranged in three groups of
four, or three tetrads. The division into
tetrads, however, appears nowhere else.
It arose, in my opinion, from the third
article and the second half of the second
appearing as though composed of four
members each. Kattenbusch in his *Programme* thinks otherwise, but in his chief
work[1] his statements on the point are
modified. I cannot, however, convince
myself that twelve divisions were originally intended.[2] No one who wanted to
construct a creed with twelve articles in
three main divisions would have been so
clumsy as to divide it into $1 + 7 + 4$, or,
rather, $2 + 6 + 4$. At all events the legend
did not originate in connexion with the

---

[1] S. 81 ff.

[2] Cf. Loofs, *I. d. GgA.* 1894, S. 675.

later and longer Roman creed, that is, the South Gallican or our present Apostles' Creed, for it already appears in the manuscript of the shorter symbol which Swainson first published, and is also proved elsewhere to apply to this creed.   Rufinus, however, who wrote later, knows nothing about it;[1] all that he knows is the common composition of the Roman symbol by the Apostles soon after Pentecost and before the separation.   But he refers this legend to a *traditio maiorum*.   It was doubtless, therefore, in existence from the beginning of the fourth century.   Both Ambrose and Rufinus testify, moreover, that the Roman Church preserved the exact words of the Apostles' Creed with the most scrupulous

---

[1] According to Kattenbusch, Rufinus wrote somewhat earlier than the author of the *Explanatio*.   See also *Expos. in Symbol. Apost.* Praef.

THE APOSTLES' CREED 19

fidelity.[1] The Apostolic origin of this symbol is independently asserted by Jerome,[2] by the Roman bishops Celestin I.

[1] Rufin. *l.c.* p. 17 : "Verum priusquam incipiam de ipsis sermonum virtutibus disputare, illud non importune commonendum puto, quod in diversis ecclesiis aliqua in his verbis inveniuntur adiecta. In ecclesia tamén urbis Romae hoc non deprehenditur factum, quod ego propterea esse arbitror, quod neque haeresis ulla illic sumpsit exordium, et mos ibi servatus antiquus, eos, qui gratiam baptismi suscepturi sunt, publice, id est, fidelium populo audiente, symbolum reddere (see Augustine, *Confess.* viii. c. 2) ; et utique adiectionem unius saltem sermonis eorum, qui praecesserunt in fide, non admittit auditus." Ambrose, *Ep.* 42 *ad Siric. P.* n. 5 (*Opp.* T. ii. P. i. p. 1125, ed Migne) : Credatur symbolo apostolorum, quod ecclesia Romana intemeratum semper custodit et servat." Ambrose, *Explanat. Symb.* in Caspari, ii. S. 56, according to a quotation from Rev. 22. 18 ff. : "Si unius apostoli scripturis nihil est detrahendum, nihil addendum, quemadmodum nos symbolo, quod accepimus ab apostolis traditum atque compositum, nihil debemus detrahere, nihil adiungere. Hoc autem est symbolum, quod Romana ecclesia tenet, ubi primus apostolorum Petrus sedit, et communem sententiam eo detulit."

[2] *Ep. ad Pammach. de errorib. Joannis Hierosol.* n. 28 (*Opp.* T. ii. p. 386, ed. Migne).

(422-431), Sixtus III. (431-440), Leo I. (440-461), by Vigilius of Thapsus, and in the *Sacramentarium Gelasianum*.[1] The belief in the Apostolic origin of the creed must therefore be regarded as originating in the Roman Church. Finally, it may be added that Augustine must also be claimed as a witness for this shorter Roman symbol. Although he was first a presbyter and then a bishop in a provincial church, in which the recognised and official symbol was one which varied considerably from the Roman, yet as a pupil of Ambrose, and as one who was baptized in the church at Milan, he held to the Roman symbol, with which, according to the *Explanatio Symboli*, the Milanese symbol was identical. In the eight expositions of the creed which we

[1] References in Caspari, ii. S. 108 f. n. 78; cf. iii. S. 94 f.; Hahn, 46, n. 163.

have from him[1] he follows the Milanese form almost exclusively, and he follows it in all essential points. In view of these facts there can be no doubt that in the fourth and the first half of the fifth century the Roman Church made extensive use in the *Redditio* of a symbol, and a symbol, too, identical with the one mentioned above, and allowed of absolutely no additions to it. Ambrose was certainly not the only one[2] who expressly protested against any anti-heretical additions. He regarded it as an attack upon the Saints to take account of contemporary difficulties in the creed, however pressing these might be. "He attributed to the creed the very highest authority, higher even than that of Apostolic writings composed by individual

[1] Caspari, ii. S. 264 f. ; Hahn, § 21.
[2] Cf. Celestin's position in the Nestorian controversy.

Apostles." The epistle of Marcellus to Julius shows us that between the years 330-340 A.D., this symbol was the official one in use in Rome; but other testimonies, which still require to be criticised and sifted, take us back with a sufficient degree of certainty to the middle of the third century. Among these the most important are Novatian's tractate *De Trinitate*,[1] and the fragments from the epistles and writings of Bishop Dionysius of Rome.[2]

That the shorter Roman symbol as represented in the Epistle of Marcellus and in the *Psalterium Aethelstani* was as early as about the year 250 the predominant one in Rome, must be regarded as one of the most positive results of historical investigation. Here, however, a series

[1] Hahn, § 7.

[2] Cf. *e.g.* Athan. *De decretis synodi Nic.* c. 26.

of questions arises, the answers to which involve very complicated investigations and the combination of different facts. The most important of these questions are as follow :

1. How is the shorter Roman symbol related to the Western symbols which were used, between the years 250 and 500 (800), in the religious services of the provincial churches until they were driven out by the (Gallican) Symbolum Apostolicum and the Nicene-Constantinopolitan ?

2. How is the shorter Roman symbol related to the longer, that is to say, to the Apostles' Creed as we know it from the time of Caesarius, and why was it displaced by the latter?

3. When and where did the shorter symbol originate ?

4. How is the shorter Roman symbol

related to the Eastern pre-Constanti-nopolitan symbols?

5. How is the shorter Roman symbol related to the different forms of the Rules of Faith with which we are familiar in the first three centuries?

These five questions can be separated only *in abstracto*. As a matter of fact they are so closely interwoven, each with the others, that a definite and separate answer to every one of them is impossible. In what follows these questions will be discussed together and a general answer attempted.

III

A SURVEY of the provincial and private confessions which remain to us from the Western Church, belonging to the period from the fourth to the sixth (seventh) century,[1] enables us to make six very important observations about them :—

1. In the choice and arrangement of

[1] Hahn, §§ 20-45 ; Caspari, Bd. ii. and iii. The fullest appreciation, however, is in Kattenbusch, S. 59-215, and in the addenda, S. 392 ff. The number of symbols found is very great, and is still increasing. We know of six Italian (besides Rome, we have symbols from Milan, Turin, Ravenna, Aquileia, and possibly also Florence), African (but none from Sardinia, for the very important one of the date 340-360, which Caspari has discussed [ii. S. 128 f.], can scarcely be attributed

the single parts they all exhibit the same fundamental type as the shorter Roman symbol.

2. The shorter a Western symbol is, the more closely it approaches the shorter Roman symbol.   The shortest symbols of the provincial churches of the West are almost, if not altogether, identical with it.

3. The later a Western symbol is, the more it varies, as a rule in consequence of additions,[1] from the shorter Roman.   With the exception of a few expressions, like the anti-modalistic " invisibili et impassibili,"

to that country; see Kattenbusch, S. 202 f.).   There are also Spanish, Gallican (South Gallican and Frankish, also one from Treves), and Irish.

[1] Hardly ever by omissions; on the symbol of Venantius Fortunatus, printed in Hahn, § 27, see Kattenbusch, S. 130 ff.   The question of alleged omissions in the Western symbols may be put aside in view of the uncertainty of the tradition.

added to the "omnipotente," in the first
article of the symbol of the church of
Aquileia; the plerophoric "huius," as an
addition to "carnis," in the third article
of the same symbol; the position of
"remissionem peccatorum, resurrectionem
carnis et vitam aeternam per sanctam
ecclesiam" in the Carthaginian Church
(this arrangement, however, may be explained otherwise), none of these additions
are of a directly polemical nature, but
are to be regarded as completions and
extensions held to be necessary in the
interest of a clear understanding of the
Creed. With these may be compared the
manifold and various additions to the first
article of the old symbol, for example :[1]
the formula "natus de Spiritu Sancto ex
Virgine Maria," in the symbol of Aquileia

[1] Hahn, § 42.

and Ravenna; the formula "conceptus de Spiritu Sancto, natus ex Virgine M." in the symbol of Faustus of Rietz; the differen tiation of "crucifixus" into "passus . . . crucifixus" in the later symbols; the addi tion of "catholicam," in the third article in the Spanish and Carthaginian symbols as well as in that of Nicetas; the addi tion of "vitam aeternam" for example, in Augustine's symbol and in Faustus of Rietz; and so on. The fundamental character of the symbols is not altered by such additions, as they are not of a speculative or dogmatic nature.

4. The majority of the additions which the Western symbols exhibit are of such a character that they may be regarded as intermediate steps between the shorter and longer Roman symbol. This con- sideration, however, is not so important as

the fact that the great provincial churches of the West in the third and fourth centuries, by the additions which they severally made, stamped the symbols with a definite character. Four such types can be readily distinguished, namely, the Italian, the African, the Gallican, which includes the Irish, and the Spanish.[1] As for the Gallican type which is seen in our Apostles' Creed, one of its distinguishing features is that it is characterised by such historical additions as are to be found in the earlier Oriental Rules of Faith or symbols, as the case may be, such as "creator of heaven and earth," "suffered," "died," "descended into hell"; and also the predicate "catholic."   The Gallican type in its

---

[1] Kattenbusch, S. 189 ff., 194 ff. makes no distinction between the last two, and recognises only one type in Western Europe ; but this view is not correct.

final form is not in every respect the richest or the longest of the Western symbols; but in so far as its historical contents are concerned, it certainly is so. What gives it its peculiar character is the fact that with the richest material contents it lacks all those finishing touches or elements of accurate definition which are present in other symbols of provincial churches, such as "invisibilem et impassibilem" in the first article; "omnium creaturarum visibilium et invisibilium conditorem" and "unum," in the first and second; "Deum" in the second; "resurrexit vivus, omnium peccatorum, cum gloria venturus, per baptismum," in the third; "huius carnis, etc." In these important respects the final form of the Gallican type, that is, of our Apostles' Creed, has completely preserved the distinguishing features of the old

Roman symbol. It exhibits the same compact and severe style, and nevertheless also preserves all the significant historical features that became attached to the Symbolum Romanum in the course of its career. The Gallican Apostles' Creed also exhibits the same classical elaboration as its Roman predecessor, and like it was regarded as possessing the same ecumenical authority.

5. The less any church was influenced by the church at Rome, the more significant become the progressive variations of its creed from the shorter Roman symbol. The symbols of the Gallican Church are relatively far removed from it.

6. If all the Western symbols be reduced to an archetype, and the differences be disregarded, we arrive without difficulty at the shorter Roman creed.

What conclusions are we to draw from these observations?   The evidence justifies the assertions (1) that the shorter Roman symbol was the source of all the Western confessions of faith; and (2) that the longer Roman symbol was gradually developed from the other, and as a consequence also preserved the same attributes as originally characterised the shorter symbol.   But the process did not take place in Rome.

From the first conclusion we may reasonably infer that the shorter Roman symbol must have originated considerably earlier than the middle of the third century. Otherwise how can we explain the fact that all the Western churches originally used the same symbol, and that the African Church, for example, had already developed its own special type, before the year 250,

upon the foundation afforded by the old
Roman symbol ?[1]   Accordingly we must
refer the Roman symbol to a date at
least as early as the year 200, which
admits of positive proof from the writings
of Tertullian.   Moreover, this conclusion
is established by a comparison between
the shorter Roman symbol and all the
Western confessions of faith on the one
side, and the provincial and private symbols
of the East on the other ; and, further, by
a comparison of the shorter Roman symbol
with the different editions of the Rule of
Faith up to the middle of the third century.

The Eastern baptismal confessions
are distinguished one and all by great
flexibility, by freedom in form, and by
richness of expression.[2]   As the Eastern

---

[1] Cyprian, Hahn, §§ 28, 29.

[2] See Hahn, *op. cit.* pp. 61 ff., pp. 183 ff.; Caspari,

Church never knew anything of any of the creeds having been composed by the Apostles, it always dealt with them in a much freer spirit, and in its baptismal confession gave expression at one and the same time to its interest in speculative theology and to its horror of every kind of heresy. It was mostly in the East that heresy originated. Thus the Eastern Church often puts dogmatic in the place of historical expressions, omits important passages, largely extends others by additional and preliminary matter, and interpolates anti‑Gnostic, anti‑Monarchian, anti‑Modalistic, anti‑Arian, anti‑Semiarian, anti‑Marcellian, anti‑Photinian, anti‑Pneumatomachian, anti‑Apollinarian, and other

op. cit. ii. S. 112 ff., iii. S. 46 f. ; Swainson, *op. cit.* p. 60 ; Hort, *Two Dissertations*, ii., On the Constantinopolitan Creed and other Eastern Creeds of the Fourth Century, 1876, p. 73 ; and, above all, Kattenbusch, S. 216 ff.

observations. "The Oriental symbols frequently exhibit in their separate articles a greater or less freedom of form, whether by inserting dogmatic in place of simple historical expressions or by uniting the two, or by expressing the article in question in a somewhat fuller manner, or, finally, by making one or more additions not of a distinctly anti-heretical character. . . . Further, we often find that they contain whole articles wanting in the Western baptismal confessions. . . . As a general result the Eastern confessions exhibit, some in a higher and some in a less degree, a subjective, reflective and dogmatic character. They wear, moreover, a more or less parti-coloured appearance, and are more or less prolix, diffuse and verbose." Lastly, catechetical instruction in doctrine, which, as is well known, was an accompaniment of the baptismal confession in the East, was much more strongly influenced by dogmatico-polemical theories than in the West. In the Eastern Church the symbol was accordingly in a constant condition of flux and movement. Not until the adoption of the Nicene-Constantinopolitan Creed was this state of things altered, and not even then was it completely altered. The Nicene Creed alone did not do it. From about the year 430 onwards this latter symbol supplanted the others in such parts of the territory of the orthodox Church as lay beyond the imperial jurisdiction. From that time the Byzantine Church became the home of severe conservatism in regard to the Creed, as up to the present day it has clung, persistently and exclusively, to the Nicene Creed. This state of things, which lasted in the East up to the middle of the fifth century, renders it difficult to describe the general character-istics of the Eastern symbols in their universality, and to reduce them to any fundamental type. Yet this much may be said : (1) That a considerable number of Eastern symbols—not all,[1] but certainly those of Syria and Palestine—are based on the same type ;[2] (2) that in its range and the disposition of its articles this type exhibits an affinity with the shorter Roman symbol, but also the following variations from it :[3] 1. πιστεύομεν is almost always used, and in many symbols it is

[1] See, e.g., the symbol of Gregory Thaumaturgus, Hahn, § 114.

[2] But, as Kattenbusch has proved, and as I previously maintained in my answer to Cremer's polemic (Leipzig, 1892, S. 9 ff.), there is no universal, independent Eastern type of the baptismal symbol.

[3] Caspari, ii. S. 44-88.

repeated with each article.   2. In the first
and second article ἕνα is added to θεόν and
to κύριον.   3. In the first article, God is
designated as the Creator of all things,
that is, of Heaven and Earth.   4. The
position of the words in the beginning
of the second article is as follows: καὶ εἰς
ἕνα (τὸν) κύριον Ἰησ. Χρ. τὸν υἱὸν αὐτοῦ τὸν
μονογενῆ.   In the Western symbol the
words Χρ. Ἰησ. stand first; τὸν υἱὸν αὐτοῦ
τὸν μονογενῆ follow, and only after
them comes τὸν κύριον.   This order is
almost everywhere preserved, and ἡμῶν
is added to κύριον.   5. Frequently "ἐκ
σπέρματος Δαβίδ," or something similar,
is added to the phrase γεννηθέντα κτλ.
6. In the East the separate clauses
of the second article are run together,
polysyndetically; in the West, asyndeti-
cally; there, the affirmations regarding

Christ take the form of sentences placed in juxtaposition; here, of relative sentences. 7. The article τὸν ἐπὶ Ποντίου Πιλάτου σταυρωθέντα καὶ ταφέντα is almost entirely lacking; here and there it appears in a modified form. 8. The words τῇ τρίτῃ ἡμέρᾳ are placed after ἀναστάντα. 9. Instead of ἀναβάντα, ἀνελθόντα or ἀναληφθέντα is used. 10. The article concerning the "coming again," is co-ordinated with the preceding. 11. Μετὰ δόξης or ἐνδόξως is added to πάλιν ἐρχόμενον. 12. In the third article the reading is τὸ πνεῦμα τὸ ἅγιον, or τ. ἅ. π. τὸ προφητικόν or something similar is often added. 13. The ἐκκλησία has the predicate καθολική after the other predicate ἁγία. Where the former appears in the later Western symbols, it stands after "Ecclesiam." 14. Baptism is frequently mentioned in the third article.

15. The words ζωὴν αἰώνιον are found almost everywhere.

All these characteristics, however, attach to a set of symbols dependent on the symbol of Nicaea, or, as the case may be, on that on which it was based (the symbol which Eusebius laid before the Council at Nicaea, usually called the Caesarean); also on Lucian's. This symbol, therefore, is not older than the beginning of the fourth century. The assertion would, of course, be open to challenge if the symbol produced by Eusebius were the baptismal confession of the Church of Caesarea.[1] But the connexion in which Eusebius communicates the symbol in his letter to his community makes it anything but probable that it is the symbol or baptismal confes-

---

[1] As Hort and Loofs, S. 673, maintain. Both assume that the third article is abridged.

sion of that place. It ought, rather, to be regarded as a symbol which Eusebius had constructed expressly for the existing situation,[1] not, of course, *ab ovo* but according to the formulas familiar at Antioch or, as the case may be, in the schools of Origen and Lucian.[2] That the congregation at Caesarea in the course of its instruction heard the faith which Eusebius here formulated is certain; but whether, over and above the baptismal confession, it possessed a definite creed consisting of three divisions is very questionable. Any such contention is strongly rebutted by the fact that in Eusebius' formula the third article simply consists of πιστεύομεν καὶ εἰς ἓν πνεῦμα ἅγιον.

[1] This may be inferred from the predicates applied to Christ : the series beginning with τὸν τοῦ θεοῦ λόγον is evidently made for the situation.

[2] See his symbol.

The assumption that Eusebius made any omission from the church confession is a very dangerous one to make. There is also the fact that a long-winded sentence follows,[1] ending in the general order to baptize. Eusebius regards this as belonging to the confession of faith as much as what preceded it : τούτων ἕκαστον εἶναι καὶ ὑπάρχειν πιστεύοντες, πατέρα ἀληθῶς πατέρα καὶ υἱὸν ἀληθῶς υἱὸν καὶ πνεῦμα ἅγιον ἀληθῶς πνεῦμα ἅγιον, καθὼς ὁ κύριος ἡμῶν ἀποστέλλων εἰς τὸ κήρυγμα τοὺς ἑαυτοῦ μαθητὰς εἶπε· πορευθέντες μαθητεύσατε πάντα τὰ ἔθνη, βαπτί-ζοντες αὐτοὺς εἰς τὸ ὄνομα τοῦ πατρὸς κτλ. This is evidently the reason why Eusebius as well as Lucian went on to the baptismal confession and repeated it *in extenso*; he felt the necessity of presenting his new formula as a paraphrase of the formula

---

[1] Cp. Lucian's symbol.

known to the community.   But if the
Caesarean symbol is not one framed for
a particular community, then we know
absolutely nothing of any definite, detailed,
ancient communal symbols in the East
of any date preceding the Nicene Creed.
This negative conclusion is confirmed by
four considerations : (1) by the curious
symbol of Gregory Thaumaturgus,[1] and
the equally curious one of Aphraates.[2]
The argument seems to me unassailable
that, where such "symbols" as these can
be constructed, there is as yet no communal
symbol, such as the Roman, in existence ;
and Gregory knew the Eastern Church
from Pontus to Egypt.   (2) By the free
and easy way in which the symbols were
formed and also accepted in the East.

[1] Hahn, § 114.
[2] Kattenbusch, S. 249.

With pain and astonishment we see this process going on in the fourth and down to the middle of the fifth century. If any old symbols had been in existence, which had come down from previous generations, how could this state of chaotic confusion and lack of reverence in the formation and acceptance of creeds in the East be explained? (3) By the above-mentioned typical similarity of structure exhibited in the Eastern symbols of the fourth century, where the type of the Lucian-Eusebean-Nicene creed is almost the only one which emerges. (4) By the uncertainty about the third article which prevailed in the East up to the middle of the fourth century. Even as late as the first Antiochian formula of the year 341 it runs as follows: εἰ δὲ δεῖ προσθεῖναι πιστεύομεν καὶ περὶ σαρκὸς ἀναστάσεως κ. ζωῆς αἰωνίου.

In connexion with this last point I may observe that the construction of the old Roman symbol is perfectly clear. It is based on the baptismal formula with its three divisions. The first division is defined by the words, "God Almighty"; the second is characterised by the phrases "Only Begotten Son" and "Our Lord," as well as by the historical account which it gives; the third is conceived of as a gift, and hence three further blessings are associated with it, which together express the content of the salvation which faith brings. Of the thirty Eastern confessions of faith from the fourth century which come into question more than two-thirds contain either no third article at all or else only a bare confession of belief in the Holy Ghost. Putting aside the symbols derived from the Nicene-Constantinopolitan,[1] and also the obviously abridged symbols mentioned by Hahn, §§ 71, 72,[2] we find that the only symbol containing the third article in a complete form, or the more than complete form which mentions Baptism, is that in the seventh book of the *Apostolic Constitutions*, in the symbol handed by Arius to the Emperor, in that of Cyril of Jerusalem, in the symbol of Salamis (which developed into the Constantinopolitan), and in the longer symbol of Epiphanius.[3] These five symbols evidently go back to one common root, which is most visible in Cyril's form, although it certainly does not easily lend itself to reconstruction.   But in the close affinity which it exhibits with the old Roman

---

[1] To which those mentioned by Hahn, §§ 68, 69, 70, belong.   [2] As against Kattenbusch, i. S. 330.

[3] Hahn, § 68.

symbol this very symbol takes precedence of all the rest. The relationship is so close that Cyril's symbol can only be the daughter or the sister of the Roman one. That it can have been the mother is out of the question, as the Roman symbol undoubtedly reveals an older and simpler form. Hitherto there has been no reason for regarding it as even a sister, for the date of this set of Palestino-Syrian symbols is not earlier than the beginning of the fourth century, whilst we can certainly place the old Roman symbol a century earlier. Now, as regards the more than twenty Eastern symbols which possess only a rudimentary third article or none at all, it is clear from the way in which christological attributes are accumulated, even in the oldest of them, that we are dealing with symbols of late origin. Still,

however, the formula θεὸς πατὴρ παντοκράτωρ, and the structure of the christological section, unmistakably exhibit a
certain affinity with the Roman symbol.
Moreover they almost all possess, in
common with the former group, additions
to the first article, as well as the ἕνα in
the first and second.   Finally, there is a
certain grammatical and literary character
common to them all.   Hence the simplest
solution of the problem presented by the
relation between the Eastern confessions
of faith of the fourth century and the old
Roman symbol, is to say that, whilst there
was no established baptismal confession
of faith in the East in the third century,
there was, however, an old, flexible
"christological rule," and also old, cere-
monial or polemical formulas of belief in
One God the Creator, and in His Only

Son Christ. Apart from the singular confession of Gregory Thaumaturgus, the venturesome character of which is apparent in the very extravagances of the legend connected with it, we may say that it was towards the end of the third century, probably in the school of Lucian, at all events at some point in Syria-Palestine, that the formation of symbols began in the East, where men—first, it seems, in theological circles—had come to know and value the Roman symbol. At the period of the struggles with Paul of Samosata other features of the Roman Church also came to be appreciated. The direct and full acceptance of the Roman symbol was, however, hindered by (1) the circumstance that the christological section of the Roman symbol came into conflict with a christological type already estab-

4

lished; (2) by the desire to give fuller expression to the "higher christology" in the creed.   It was not until the time of the Arian controversy that fixed symbols in the East began to be formed.   The type[1] that was apparently, at least, the most frequent up to the year 381, was that with the short third article (in "the," or, as the case might be, the "One," "Holy Ghost"; or also, in some instances, with additions such as "Who spake by the Prophets"); whilst the type which, in the third article, is in essential agreement with the old Roman symbol came to the front in the Jerusalem-Salamis symbol, and in that contained in the seventh book of the *Apostolic Constitutions*,[2] and

[1] Lucian, Eusebius, Arius, § 117, the Nicene, the whole of the Antiochian and Sirmian symbols, etc.

[2] How old this symbol may be is a question.

then gradually gained the supremacy through the Nicene - Constantinopolitan Creed.

The question may be asked whether this conclusion is not upset by an examination of the Rules of Faith, and the fragments of those rules and formula-like sentences with which we are familiar as belonging to the Eastern half of the Church from the middle of the first to the middle of the third century. This is the opinion entertained by Caspari, Zahn, Loofs, and many others, and formerly I, too, shared it. The idea is that we must take an Eastern symbol or, to be more precise, a symbol from Asia Minor, and relate the old Roman symbol to it as daughter or sister. The assumption rests principally if not exclusively on what we find in Clement of Alexandria,

Irenaeus, Justin and Ignatius. The opponents of this view argue briefly as follows:— "The writings of Justin, who was baptized in Ephesus about the year 130, show us that he assumes the existence of a symbol which on the one hand much resembles the old Roman, and on the other is most characteristically distinguished from it. These distinguishing marks also appear in the majority of the later Eastern symbols ('Ιησοῦς Χριστός not X. 'I.; σταυρωθεὶς ἐπὶ Π. Π. not ἐπὶ Π. Π στ.; ἀποθανόντα; πάλιν μετὰ δόξης, etc.); further, they are also to be found in the formulas of Irenaeus, who employs others as well as ἕνα, ποιητὴν οὐρανοῦ καὶ γῆς, and in certain peculiarities of style which may also be shown to exist in Eastern symbols of the fourth century. Some of these can be traced back as far

as Ignatius, nay, even to the Epistles of
St. Paul, or, in fact, to the New Testament in general.   Finally, it follows from
what Clement says that in his time there
existed a formal and fixed baptismal confession in Alexandria.   In the East, then,
there existed in the second century a
fixed symbol, or, rather, many symbols,
related to the Roman symbol, but inde-
pendent of it.   The history of Eastern
symbols may therefore be traced well into
the second century, and this history,
accordingly, though latent in the third
century, was still existent.   The Roman
symbol at best is contemporaneous with
the Asiatic or Syrian ; more probably it is
later; and this Asiatic or Syrian symbol
leaves it free to the critic to assign it to
the years 120–130, 100–120, or 70–100."
Such is the argument.

. Against it four considerations may be urged :

(1) The fact that single sentences seem to be echoes of the symbol or tally with it offers no guarantee that they themselves derive from one symbol.   Before any symbol existed God was παντοκράτωρ ; Jesus Christ was called " the Only Begotten Son, our Lord "; he was proclaimed as " born of the Holy Ghost of the Virgin Mary," as having suffered under Pontius Pilate, and as coming to judge the quick and the dead.

(2) Formula - like sentences, if not obviously a part of the baptismal formula, need not necessarily have originated in a baptismal confession, even though they be identical with the sentences of that confession.   The oldest tradition gave a fixed or, as the case may be, a more fixed

shape to "The Faith," not only in the form of a baptismal confession and for the purposes of baptism, but also in (a) liturgical sentences, (b) formulas of exorcism, (c) precepts concerning faith and morals, and (d) historical summaries, and that, too, with a view to the most diverse objects (instruction, apologetics, polemics, religious worship). As illustrating (a) we may take the prayers in the *Didaché;* (b) statements in Justin and others; (c) Hermas, *Mand.* I and *Didaché* 1-6; (d) I Cor. xv. I ff., Mark xvi. 9 ff. The words of John xvii. 3 ἵνα γινώσκωσι σὲ τὸν μόνον ἀληθινὸν θεὸν καὶ ὃν ἀπέστειλας Ἰ. Χρ. were in the middle of the second century as much a formula of faith as Hermas, *Mand.* I πρῶτον πάντων πίστευσον, ὅτι εἷς ἐστιν θεός κτλ., yet they have nothing to do with the baptismal formula. Such

passages as Ephes. iv. 9 furnished themes
for homiletical discourses ; formulas were
also set up which led from the confession
of the One God to the chief practical
commandments ; of these some fine and
powerful examples are found in *Mand.* 1 ff.
and *Didaché* 1 ff.   Finally, the preaching
of Christ is not unfrequently attached,
on the foundation of numerous Pauline
passages, to a confession of belief in the
One God, without any mention of the
Holy Spirit, of the Church, or of Christian
blessings.

(3) In particular, the preaching of
Christ, apart from the detailed form which
it received in the Gospels,[1] also underwent
various longer or shorter epitomisations,[2]

---

[1] Luke i. 4.

[2] See the above-mentioned fragments 1 Cor. xv. and
Mark xvi. 9.

which took a fixed form without being placed in a Trinitarian framework. These epitomisations proceeded on various plans : (a) the mere chronicle, (b) the chronicle with proofs attached, (c) the plan of fulfilled prophecy, (d) the plan κατὰ σάρκα κατὰ πνεῦμα, (e) the plan of the first and second coming, (f) the plan καταβάς—ἀναβάς. All these plans, in part united with one another, issued in affirmations of a character relatively fixed, even if capable of being modified.

(4) Out of the great number of predicates attached to God, Christ, and the Spirit, some which were in general use very soon came to the front, apart from the detailed Trinitarian confession. Those chiefly used in connexion with God are, εἷς, παντοκράτωρ, πατήρ, δεσπότης and Creator, with additions ; with Christ, ὁ υἱὸς τοῦ θεοῦ, ὁ

κύριος, σωτήρ, διδάσκαλος, μονογενής, εἷς, λόγος ;
with the Holy Ghost ἅγιος, προφητικός.   In
the same way, out of the great number of
blessings which the Christian faith affords,
some are named with especial frequency,
such as ἄφεσις ἁμαρτιῶν (with or without
mention of baptism), ζωή (αἰώνιος), ἀνάστα-
σις (with or without τῆς σαρκός), γνῶσις,
ἀφθαρσία, etc.   Everything thus variously
produced was regarded as " the Faith,"
"the Rule of Faith," "Kerugma" (or "Pro-
clamation "), " Truth," " Rule of Truth,"
μάθημα, παράδοσις, παραδοθείς λόγος, διδαχή,
etc.

A consideration of the facts contained
in the foregoing, the truth of which no
scholar will question, must make us very
cautious in arguing from formula-like confessional sentences to a formulated baptis-
·mal confession in three parts.   Caution of

this kind seems to be everywhere wanting at the present time, as is seen, for example, in Zahn's treatise on the Apostles' Creed (1893) and in the way in which it has been received by the most distinguished students in this branch of learning. No one has a right to claim a particular proposition, which forms no part of any creed framed on the Trinitarian plan, as part of a fixed baptismal confession, unless he is in a position to offer very strong evidence for his contention.

What is the net result of the "testimony" of Ignatius, Justin, Irenaeus, and Clement of Alexandria?

(1) We find that Ignatius has freely reproduced a "kerugma" of Christ which seems, in essentials, to be of a fairly definite historical character and which contained, *inter alia*, the Virgin Birth, Pontius

Pilate and the ἀπέθανεν.   There is no trace of any evidence, however, that it was part of any creed based on the Trinitarian plan.

(2) As to Justin we find (*a*) that he knew of a definite christological "kerugma," and used it again and again; this was closely related to the second article of the Roman symbol, although quite inde-pendent of it, and it even exhibits many of the characteristic peculiarities of the later Eastern symbols; (*b*) that with him this "kerugma" forms no part of any baptismal symbol, that is to say, is not a formal second article; (*c*) that with him the baptismal formula was not developed into a symbol at all, except that the three Persons were described as follows: ὁ πατὴρ τῶν ὅλων καὶ δεσπότης θεός, Ἰησοῦς Χριστὸς ὁ σταυρωθεὶς ἐπὶ Ποντίου Πιλάτου, τὸ πνεῦμα

ἅγιον ὃ διὰ τῶν προφητῶν προεκήρυξε τὰ κατὰ τὸν Ἰησοῦν πάντα, or, simply, τὸ προφητικόν; any such description, however, in the baptismal formula itself, is improbable; (*d*) that it is extremely likely that the christological "kerugma" above indicated was formally stated as fulfilled prophecy, that is to say, stood as part of a plan as follows: "The Holy Ghost prophesied etc."; but we can go no farther in this direction than the assumption that Justin knew of a "kerugma"; that after the mention of πατὴρ τῶν ὅλων καὶ δεσπότης, and Jesus Christ, a "kerugma" of Christ, in the form of fulfilled prophecy or, as the case may be, in the form of a belief in the prophetic spirit, was added.   But the contention that this μάθημα was a baptismal confession, or, as the case may be, claimed to be a developed baptismal formula, and that it existed in a crystallised form at all, is unsupported by any evidence.

(3) As regards Irenaeus, (*a*) as I have shown in the first article against Zahn in the *Zeitschrift für Theologie und Kirche*, Bd. iv. S. 149 ff., we must be very cautious in drawing conclusions from his "testimonies on behalf of the baptismal confession"; a very small portion of the material which I collected from Irenaeus in the treatise on the old Roman symbol[1] is sufficient to determine the "symbol" which he employed; (*b*) according to Irenaeus i. 9, 4 baptism bestows the κανὼν τῆς ἀληθείας; this canon he himself communicates in i. 10, 1. The form in which he here produces it, supplemented by the watchwords of his theology, and given in other places with fragmentary variations,

---

[1] *Patr. App. Opp.* edit. 2, T. i. 2, pp. 123 ff.

shows that he is compiling it independently out of a large number of fixed confessional formulas of the Church. Among these may be distinguished :

1. The expanded formula of Hermas.[1]

2. The formula εἷς θεὸς παντοκράτωρ united with Johannine expressions or, as the case may be, with πεποιηκὼς τ. οὐρανὸν κ. τ. γῆν κ. τ. θαλάσσας καὶ πάντα τ. ἐν αὐτοῖς, or εἷς μονογενὴς Ἰησοῦς Χριστός.

3. A christological formula of confession (in an historical form), showing a close relation to the old Roman symbol, but a still closer one to Justin's.

4. The θεὸς πατὴρ παντοκράτωρ of the Roman symbol.

5. A formula of confession which the confession of belief in the One God and One Christ Jesus joined a confession

[1] *Mand.* 1.

of belief in the Holy Spirit, and incorporated with this confession the history of Christ as fulfilled prophecy. As we were enabled to make a similar conjecture in Justin's case, so it is probable that not only in Irenaeus' time but also in Justin's a confessional formula existed in the East containing something like the following :—ἡ εἰς ἕνα θεὸν παντοκράτορα (or εἰς τὸν πατέρα τῶν ὅλων καὶ δεσπότην θεὸν) πίστις καὶ εἰς ἕνα Ἰησοῦν Χριστὸν τὸν υἱὸν τοῦ θεοῦ, τὸν σαρκωθέντα ὑπὲρ ἡμῶν (or ὑπὲρ τῆς ἡμετέρας σωτηρίας) καὶ εἰς πνεῦμα ἅγιον, τὸ διὰ τῶν προφητῶν κεκηρυχὸς τὰς οἰκονομίας, τὴν ἐκ παρθένου γέννησιν κτλ. From this formula, which Irenaeus made the foundation of his κανῶν τῆς ἀληθείας, the historico-christological formula of confession containing the sentences about the birth, suffering under Pontius Pilate, burial, resurrection,

and coming again in glory (in finite verb
or, as the case may be, participle) is
perhaps, or even probably, to be distinguished.   Parallels are also to be found
for this formula in Justin and Ignatius or,
as the case may be, in 1 Cor. xv.   This
is as far as the material hitherto discovered will allow us to go on this subject.
That Irenaeus assumed the existence of
a symbol, or, in other words, that the
formulas (plans) indicated above were in
existence in their crystallised form, not
only cannot be demonstrated but is
entirely improbable.   Irenaeus' whole line
of argument must have issued in a
different conclusion had there existed in
a fixed form, recognised in his community,
what is necessary for his demonstration,
that " Multa," that is to say, many familiar
formulas and short statements of faith,

5

existed, but no "Multum," that is to say, that there was no symbol.   There is nothing in the objection that Tertullian proceeds in a similar way, and that he certainly assumes the Roman symbol to be already known.   Tertullian's references to a symbol are incomparably clearer.[1] But that he had to serve up to his readers as Apostolic tradition the *quid pro quo*, that is to say, formulas constructed *ad hoc*, followed from the fact that the text of the Roman symbol was insufficient for the theological and anti-Gnostic objects which he had in view.   We may, however, ask whether the Irenaeus of Asia Minor and Gaul had ever heard of the Roman symbol. In view of the distinct formula θεὸς πατὴρ παντοκράτωρ, and the way in which he uses

[1] See the evidence adduced in my above-mentioned treatise, and Kattenbusch, i. pp. 141 ff.

the Roman community as evidence in his argument for tradition, I am disposed to assume that he had.

Lastly, as regards Clement of Alexandria, there is a still unsettled controversy as to whether he does not in one place assume the existence of a fixed symbol in that city.   Even if this be so—it seems to me still extremely doubtful—there is no art which can discover how this symbol ran.   It may have been something entirely different from what we call a symbol. Therefore we may leave it out of account.

That there existed in Asia Minor, or in Syria, or, in short, in the East before the beginning of the third century, symbols used as baptismal confessions which were based upon the baptismal formula, gave the second article in the form of an historical account, and summarised in the third the blessings which faith receives, cannot be shown. To prove the existence in the East at all, in the earliest period, of any fixed crystallised confession, and therefore of a primitive Eastern symbol closely related to the old Roman one, but still independent of it, is impossible. Not only can the existence of any such primitive symbol not be proved, but it is quite improbable, as the history of the Eastern Church shows in the third century by its silence, and in the fourth by what it says. Nevertheless the result of our investigations is not merely negative. On the contrary, we can agree that those who defend the existence of a primitive typical Eastern symbol are, up to a certain point, right. There did actually exist in the East (in Asia Minor or, as the case may be, Asia Minor and Syria), as early as the beginning of the second century, *inter alia* a christological μάθημα, which is most intimately related to the second article of the Roman creed, and which, as regards the formulas and details peculiar to it, made its way into the Eastern symbols of the fourth century.   There existed, further, formulas referring to One God, the Creator of Heaven and Earth, and to His Incarnate Son, which also made their way, and exerted an influence on the whole process of forming symbols, including many modifications of the Roman symbols in the West.   The exclusively theological tenor of the Eastern symbols in the second article may be traced to the primitive σαρκωθέντα. Finally, there existed a formula which asserted of the holy prophetic Spirit the facts which it proclaimed in regard to Christ.   Apart from these leading formulas

the words "descensus" and "catholica"
point to the East.   But nevertheless the
great feat of having formed the symbol,
and of therewith laying the foundation
of all ecclesiastical symbols, remains the
glory of the community at Rome.

When did this happen?   We have
traced the old Roman symbol to the time
of Tertullian.   It is this symbol that he
means when he writes *de praescr. haer.* 36 :
"Si autem Italiae adjaces, habes Romam,
unde nobis quoque auctoritas praesto
est . . . videamus quid didicerit, quid
docuerit, cum Africanis quoque ecclesiis
contesserarit.   Unum deum dominum
novit, creatorem universitatis, et Christum
Jesum ex Virgine Maria filium dei
creatoris et carnis resurrectionem . . . et
ita adversus hanc institutionem neminem
recipit."   This symbol we unhesitatingly

trace back to about the middle of the second century. Had a symbol been established in Rome at the time of the fierce struggle with Gnosticism and Marcionism (about 145-190), it would have taken a different form ; on the other hand, to go back too far beyond the middle of the second century is unwise. There are a great many things in the *Shepherd* of Hermas, both as a whole and in its several parts, which would be difficult to explain if the Roman symbol had been familiar to the writer. Justin shows us that about the middle of the second century the distinction between ἐκ and διὰ Μαρίας had not yet been effected. The omission of Jesus' baptism by John, and also of the Johannine expression υἱὸς μονογενής, the omission of the chiliastic hopes, and the sharp distinction between ἀναστάντα, ἀναβάντα and καθήμενον, are facts to be seriously weighed.   In addition, the expression θεὸς πατὴρ παντοκράτωρ has no history behind it, and it gradually displaced an older expression εἰς θεὸς παντοκράτωρ.   This I have already shown in the *Zeitschrift für Theologie und Kirche,*[1] in which I refuted Zahn's hypothesis that the old Roman symbol originally began with the words πιστεύω εἰς ἕνα θεὸν παντοκράτορα.   The old Roman symbol always ran as it now runs, but the text of its first article must have made its way in opposition to an older and very wide-spread form of the confession of God as the Creator.   To Hermas the formula θεὸς πατὴρ παντοκράτωρ is as yet unknown. This also makes it probable that the symbol originated about the middle of

[1] Bd. iv. S. 130 ff.

the second century or shortly before. The text, too, of the Eastern christological μάθημα, which was presumably known to the author of the old Roman symbol, is, if it contains Jesus' Baptism by John and does not mention the Ascension, older than the Roman symbol, just as the παθόντα, ἀποθανόντα, as well as πάλιν and ἐν δόξῃ, can be put a long way back. Finally, if we examine the Roman symbol clause by clause, the following facts are established :

(1) The symbol itself is the oldest witness for the formula θεὸς πατὴρ παντοκράτωρ, which gradually superseded an older form.

(2) υἱὸς ὁ μονογενής is Johannine.

(3) The oldest and frequently recurring formula for the Virgin birth always runs γεννηθέντα ἐκ Μαρίας τῆς παρθένου. The

addition of ἐκ πνεύματος ἁγίου in the "kerugmatic" sentences is relatively late, and presumably comes from the Gospels.

(4) The ταφέντα there is in like manner late.

(5) The addition of τῇ τρίτῃ ἡμέρᾳ to ἀναστάντα. Both come from the First Epistle to the Corinthians.

(6) The special prominence given to ἀναβάντα between ἀναστάντα and καθήμενον is also relatively late, and shows a desire for completeness which is best explained by the high regard felt for the only existing account.[1]

(7) The enumeration of the blessings of salvation, as given in the third article, cannot be understood apart from the Pauline Epistles, but it lends a precision to what was taken from those Epistles by

[1] Acts i.

the particular prominence given to the Resurrection as a Resurrection of the body. The fact that in the Roman symbol older and shorter "kerugmatic" sentences were somewhat further developed under the influence of the New Testament writings, and particularly under that of John, the Synoptists, Paul, and probably the Acts of the Apostles, makes it unwise to trace the composition of the symbol backwards beyond the middle of the second century.

To sum up: the symbol originated in Rome about the middle of the second century. It was based upon the baptismal formula and on confessional formulas of a summarising character (such as we can identify from the New Testament and from Ignatius, Justin, and Irenaeus), which had been generally handed down, including Eastern formulas (Asia Minor, Syria), as also largely under the influence of the New Testament writings. Among these confessional formulas the most important was a christological $\mu\acute{a}\theta\eta\mu\alpha$ of fairly fixed form, yet capable of being added to and modified. Its main outlines, I presume, are recognisable. In Rome itself the Roman symbol was never altered. It made its way into the Western provinces from the end of the second century onwards, without raising any claim to have been, in the strictest sense, composed by the Apostles. That is why it underwent different modifications in those provinces. (In Rome it was not until some time between 250 and 350 onwards that it was designated as Apostolic in the strict sense of the term.) Amongst these modifications, those became historically the most important which derive from the primitive confessional formulas of the East or, as the case may be, the μάθημα, namely, "creator of heaven and earth," "suffered," "died," "descended into hell," "eternal life," besides the "catholica"— these are just the modifications traceable in the Gallic symbols which issue in our Apostles' Creed—in addition, the "conceptus," which is obscure in its origin and otherwise of little importance, and, most perplexing of all, the "communio sanctorum." In this connexion may rightly be borne in mind the particularly close relations existing between Southern Gaul and the East. But an historical circumstance of very special importance seems also to have played a part. Hitherto I have said nothing about

the Symbol of Nicetas.[1]   Morin[2] has made
it very probable that Nicetas means the
Nicetas of Remesiana in Dacia, the friend
of Paulinus of Nola.[3]   The symbol which
he adduces can unhappily be no longer
reconstructed in detail from his *Explanatio;* but so much is certain, that it
is closely related to the old Roman
symbol.   What is much more interesting,
however, is the fact that throughout (partly
word by word) he explains it by the
catechising activity of Cyril of Jerusalem,
and in this connexion brings in the
sentence " Ergo in hac una ecclesia
crede te communionem consecuturum esse
sanctorum."   Whether the catchwords
belong to Nicetas' symbol is very question-

[1] Caspari, *Anecdota*, S. 341 ff. ; Kattenbusch, i. pp.
108 ff. ; Hahn, § 25.

[2] *Rev. bénédict.* Tom. xi. Febr.

[3] His date is the beginning of the fifth century.

able (to me improbable); but in any case,
so far as their origin is concerned, their
presence there could be explained by
reference to Cyril's words. As there is
a certain relationship between Nicetas'
symbol and the Gallican (we may ask
whether his symbol was not even influenced by Cyril's), and as connexions
between Gaul and Pannonia are not lacking, the possibility presents itself—more
than this I will not say at present—of
conceiving the Gallican symbol, with the
clause "communio sanctorum," that is to
say, our Apostles' Creed, as having arisen
about the year 500 under the indirect
influence of Cyril's catechising (carried on
throughout the Remesiana in Pannonia
and Aquileia).   Loofs[1] and I[2]   have

[1] Loofs, S. 677.
[2] *Theologische Literaturzeitung*, 1894, Kol. 582.

80   THE APOSTLES' CREED

indicated this possibility independently of each other. At all events a piece of ecclesiastical "ecumenicity" adheres to a part of the additions which distinguish our Apostles' Creed from the old Roman symbol. If "communio sanctorum" is not to be traced to Cyril, but to be regarded, rather, as a product of chance, it must be understood in Augustine's sense (*i.e.*, the Church as the community of the Saints), or, with Faustus of Rietz, as a fellowship with the martyrs and specially holy men. Zahn[1] has recently suggested another derivation, namely, that "communio sanctorum" is equivalent to τὴν κοινωνίαν τῶν ἁγίων, the latter meaning "sacramenta." *Sub judice lis est.*"

That the Roman Church after the be-

[1] *Op. cit.* pp. 82 ff.

ginning of the sixth century gradually let itself be separated from and finally robbed of the symbol which it had previously guarded so faithfully, is a striking pheno-menon which has not yet had its causes clearly explained.   Meanwhile, however, Caspari[1] has made some very important contributions towards a solution of the problem.   The most critical fact that it was not in the first instance the longer (Gallican) daughter edition (our Apostles' Creed) which displaced the mother symbol but the Nicene-Constantinopolitan, which from the beginning of the sixth century first took the place of the shorter one in Rome in the *Traditio* and *Redditio symboli*, while in the baptismal interroga-tion the old Roman still remained in use. The displacement of the old Roman symbol

[1] *Op. cit.* ii. S. 114 f., iii. S. 201 f., 230 f.

by the Constantinopolitan becomes very intelligible, as soon as we consider the conditions of the time.   From the end of the fifth century, under the dominion of Odoacer and the Ostrogoths, Arianism had impinged upon the Roman Church, and had become a danger to it. By way of counteracting it the Roman Church will have resolved to give up its ancient practice, so as in its very baptismal formula to express its disavowal of Arianism.   When three centuries later the church returned to a shorter symbol, the old Roman one had already retreated into the background, and the new Roman symbol, which was, in fact, the Gallican, the Apostles' Creed, possessed the recommendation of having a series of elaborations which were wanting in the earlier one, and which now seemed indispensable.

But we may probably also assume—direct information we have, of course, none—that the Roman Church would have difficulties about accepting the Frankish symbol as a baptismal one, had it not been recognised as an old acquaintance. It is, moreover, very probable that there was still enough historical tradition present in Rome to allow of the Frankish confession reminding people of one that was old and once highly honoured. The differences were overlooked or else not regarded as considerable. Thus the legend which had encircled the old symbol with a halo of glory awoke again around the new one, and again and for a long time became a power in the Church. Not until the age of the Renaissance and the Reformation was it exploded.

IV

In interpreting the Apostles' Creed historically the foregoing observations supply us with the rule that those portions of it which were already a part of the old Roman confession are to be explained from the theology of the later Apostolic and post-Apostolic ages, not simply, as some claim, from the New Testament. This explanation must take note of the fact that the symbol is an elaborated baptismal formula,[1] and therefore it must not be regarded in its ancient

---

[1] "Amplius aliquid respondentes, quam dominus in evangelio determinavit" (Tertul. *De coron. mil.* 3).

form as in any way an expression of intra-church polemics, but rather as a Christian confession, framed with the object of giving instruction in Christianity, as distinguished from Judaism and Heathenism.[1] In the course of history, the theological explanation of the symbol naturally keeps pace, in the main, with the general development of dogmatics and theology. But the distinction between theological rules of faith and a confession serving for Christian instruction is always clear to Western consciousness, and is characteristically reflected in the *Explanationes Symboli*. As regards the phrases which we find in the Apostles' Creed but not in the old Roman one, we

[1] Upon the use of the symbol as the foundation of catechetical instruction, cp. Zezschwitz, *Katechetik*, ii. i. S. 73-139. See also the work on the *Disciplina Arcani*.

must ascertain when, where, and under
what conditions they first appeared. Of
most of them it may be said that they
are a natural elaboration of the old
symbol, that they do not alter its character, that they contain only the common
faith of the Church, even of the Church of
the second century, and that at the end of
the second century they were also known
to the churches of the West, even though
they had not yet found a stable place in
any of the provincial symbols.[1]   Two only
of the additions made cannot be so regarded ; these are the phrases "descendit
ad inferna" in the second article, and
"sanctorum communionem" in the third.
"Catholicam" is in a different case.[2]   The

---

[1] Zezschwitz, *op. cit.* 116 f.

[2] *Ibid.* 118 f.; Caspari, iii. S. 149 f.   On the sub-
stitution of the predicate "Catholic" for "Christian,"

first phrase appears in the West at the earliest in the symbol of Aquileia as given by Rufinus.[1] The second has been discussed above. At all events. the first is so far in a better position in that there is a clear tradition supporting it, which goes back far into the second century.   In Marcion's time the "descensus ad inferos" formed a part of the church teaching.[2]   I am therefore disposed to believe that what led to the acceptance of this part of the creed was less any anti-Apollinarian interest, or any definite theory as to the condition of the souls in the kingdom of the dead, than the endeavour to give as complete an account

which already appears in the pre-Reformation symbols, see Zezschwitz, p. 127.

[1] Cp. the fourth Sirmian formula in Hahn, § 93.

[2] Caspari, iii. S. 206 f.; Zezschwitz, S. 117 f., 119 f., 125 f.

as possible of the history of Christ's pas-
sion and his glory. The oldest inter-
preters make "descendit" equivalent to
"sepultus." Nevertheless, even from the
point of view of comparative criticism,
both additions will, on account of their
dubious meaning, be allowed to be
failures. Even in modern times they
are explained quite differently by different
parties in the Church.[1]

[1] On the principal Articles of Faith in the Middle
Ages and in the Reformation churches, see Zezschwitz,
p. 129 f. On the various attempts from Calixtus and
Lessing down to Grundvig and his followers to enhance
the authority of the Apostles' Creed and raise it to a
position side by side with, nay, above, the New Testament, whether in a syncretistic, eirenic, antibiblical, or
conservative-catholic interest, cp. the literature cited
ibid. p. 77 f., and in Kattenbusch, *op. cit.* i. pp. 1 ff.
The latter gives a detailed survey of the entire literature
of the subject.

Printed by R. & R. CLARK, LIMITED, *Edinburgh.*